An Especially Tricky People

Doonesbury books by G. B. Trudeau

Still a Few Bugs in the System
The President Is a Lot Smarter Than You Think
But This War Had Such Promise
Call Me When You Find America
Guilty, Guilty, Guilty!
"What Do We Have for the Witnesses, Johnnie?"
Dare To Be Great, Ms. Caucus
Wouldn't a Gremlin Have Been More Sensible?
"Speaking of Inalienable Rights, Amy . . ."
You're Never Too Old for Nuts and Berries
An Especially Tricky People
As the Kid Goes for Broke
Stalking the Perfect Tan
"Any Grooming Hints for Your Fans, Rollie?"
But the Pension Fund Was Just Sitting There
We're Not Out of the Woods Yet
A Tad Overweight, but Violet Eyes to Die For

In Large Format

The Doonesbury Chronicles
Doonesbury's Greatest Hits

a Doonesbury classic by

GB Trudeau.

An Especially Tricky People

An Owl Book   🦉   **Holt, Rinehart and Winston / New York**

Published by Holt, Rinehart and Winston, 383 Madison Avenue,
New York, New York 10017.

Published simultaneously in Canada by Holt, Rinehart and
Winston of Canada, Limited.

Library of Congress Catalog Card Number: 76-45281

ISBN: 0-03-020681-2

Printed in the United States of America

The cartoons in this book have appeared in newspapers
in the United States and abroad under the auspices of
Universal Press Syndicate.

10 9 8 7 6 5 4

AS FAR AS DETENTE IS CON—
CERNED, WE'LL JUST HAVE TO
SEE WHAT DEVELOPS. I'M SURE
MY CHINESE HOSTS WOULD BE AS
SADDENED TO SEE U.S. GUNBOATS
STEAMING UP THE YANGTZE AS
I WOULD BE.

SIR, DO YOU
EXPECT TO CON—
TINUE INGESTING
RECREATIONAL
DRUGS DURING
YOUR STAY IN
CHINA?

ABSOLUTELY—
I INTEND TO
STRESS CON—
TINUITY IN
MY PERSONAL
HABITS!

I HAVE ALSO BEEN
ASSURED BY MY ATTENDING
MEDICAL OFFICER THAT HE'LL
BE ABLE TO FILL THE PHARMA—
CEUTICAL REQUIREMENTS OF
THE LIAISON OFFICE SOCIAL
FUNCTIONS.

BUT, SIR, AS
YOU MUST KNOW,
YOUR CHINESE
HOSTS FROWN
ON ALL FORMS
OF EXCESS.

MY CHINESE
HOSTS CAN
GO SUCK
EGGS.

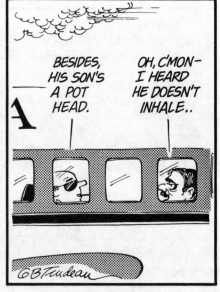

A LIGHT DRIZZLE GREETED THE NEW CHIEF OF THE U.S. MISSION AS HIS PLANE TOUCHED DOWN HERE AT PEKING INTERNATIONAL AIRPORT..

THE PASSENGER DOOR OF THE AIRCRAFT HAS BEEN OPENED, AND CHINESE OFFICIALS ARE NOW GATHERING ON THE RUNWAY TO MEET THE NEW TOP ENVOY.

THE GREETING IS EXPECTED TO BE STRAINED, AS AMBASSADOR DUKE IS KNOWN TO BE OPENLY SUSPICIOUS OF HIS CHINESE HOSTS.

COVER ME— I THINK I CAN MAKE THE LIMO!

BUT, SIR— IT'S ONLY AN HONOR GUARD..

TELL ME, HONEY — IS IT HARD TO CONVERSE WITH THE CHAIRMAN? I WAS TOLD HIS STROKE LEFT HIM WITH A SPEECH IMPAIRMENT..

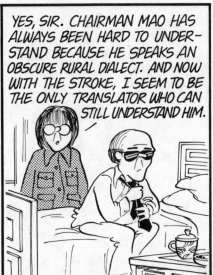

YES, SIR. CHAIRMAN MAO HAS ALWAYS BEEN HARD TO UNDERSTAND BECAUSE HE SPEAKS AN OBSCURE RURAL DIALECT. AND NOW WITH THE STROKE, I SEEM TO BE THE ONLY TRANSLATOR WHO CAN STILL UNDERSTAND HIM.

NO KIDDING?.. MAN, THAT CERTAINLY LEAVES YOU WITH A HELL OF A RESPONSIBILITY, DOESN'T IT?

YES, SIR. IN A WAY, I'M SORT OF RUNNING THE COUNTRY.

I'LL KEEP THAT IN MIND.

GBTrudeau

..AND EVEN IN THE WANING DAYS OF THE SAGA OF PATTY HEARST, THIS REPORTER REMAINS IMPRESSED BY THE PAGEANTRY AND SPECTACLE WHICH HAS COME TO CHARACTERIZE THIS MOST CELEBRATED OF ALL CRIMINAL PROCEEDINGS..

HERE IN THE COURTHOUSE, THE CORRIDORS REMAIN PACKED WITH THE HUNDREDS WHO HAVE BECOME PART OF THE UNFOLDING DRAMA— THE MARSHALS, THE LAWYERS, THE REPORTERS, THE PSYCHIATRISTS, THE DELI DELIVERY BOYS...

..AND INSIDE THE COURTROOM ITSELF, TENSION REMAINS HIGH AS BAILEY SHOWS SLIDES OF THE RUBBLE AT SAN SIMEON, AND CLIPS FROM THE MOVIE HE SAYS THE SLA REPEATEDLY FORCED PATTY TO WATCH, "CITIZEN KANE."

MEANWHILE, OUT IN THE STREET, DANCING BEARS AND JUGGLERS HAVE BECOME A FAMILIAR SIGHT..

GBTrudeau

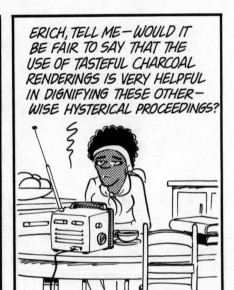

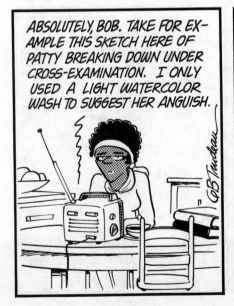

ONCE AGAIN TODAY, BAILEY HAMMERED HOME HIS KEY ARGUMENT: MIND CONTROL WAS BEHIND PATTY'S ANTI-SOCIAL BEHAVIOR IN THE HIBERNIA BANK.

PROSECUTOR BROWNING WAS CLEARLY INCREDULOUS. "BRAINWASHING?," HE LATER SCOFFED TO REPORTERS, "DRIPPING FAUCETS? C'MON! EVEN HER FIANCE, STEPHEN WEED, ADMITS PATTY HAS ALWAYS KNOWN HER OWN MIND!"

MEANWHILE, WEED HIMSELF WAS PRESIDING OVER A HASTILY CALLED PRESS CONFERENCE TODAY TO DISCUSS HIS FORMER LIFE WITH PATTY, AS REVEALED IN HIS NEW BOOK, "WEED'S-EYE VIEW."

AND THEN...CHILD-LIKE...SHE REACHED OUT AND TOUCHED MY PRINCETON WARM-UP JACKET..

THROUGHOUT THIS ARDUOUS TRIAL, F. LEE BAILEY'S STRATEGY HAS BEEN TO PORTRAY MS. HEARST AS THE VICTIM OF RELENTLESS DURESS, WHICH BENT HER MIND INTO THAT OF AN UNWITTING CRIMINAL.

TOWARD THAT END, THE INDEFATIGABLE ADVOCATE HAS USED ALL MANNER OF HISTRIONICS TO IMPRESS UPON THE JURY THE EXTENT TO WHICH HIS CLIENT HAD BEEN SUBJECTED TO PHYSICAL AND MENTAL ABUSE.

IT THUS CAME AS SMALL SURPRISE TODAY WHEN BAILEY CHOSE TO DELIVER HIS SUMMATION TO THE JURY AT THE ACTUAL SCENE OF PATTY'S CONFINEMENT..

LET ME OUT!

I CAN'T BREATHE!

GOD, IT'S HOT IN HERE!!

THE DEFENSE RESTS.

BAM! BAM!

MAY I SPEAK WITH MS. CAUCUS, PLEASE?

SPEAKING.

MS. CAUCUS, I'VE HEARD YOU'VE ASKED ZONKER HARRIS TO WORK FOR MS. SLADE! I'D ADVISE AGAINST IT. HE'S A DANGEROUS, SICK BOY, AND HE BELONGS AT HOME WHERE HE CAN BE LOOKED AFTER!

ZONKER? ARE YOU KIDDING? SAY, WHO IS THIS ANYWAY?!

A FRIEND..

ALRIGHT, **WHAT'S** GOING ON HERE?!

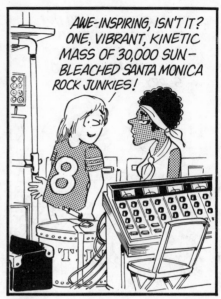

ALL RIGHT, KID, WE LOST ROUND ONE. BUT THAT DOESN'T MEAN WE'RE DOWN! WE'LL JUST TAKE THE INDEPENDENT ROUTE, OKAY?

NO. NOT OKAY.

GINNY, LOOK, WE'VE GAINED A LOT OF EXPERIENCE! I KNOW WE CAN CRANK UP A SERIOUS CAMPAIGN THIS TIME!

YOU **CAN'T** HANG IT UP NOW, GINNY! YOU WERE JUST BEGINNING TO MAKE A DIFFERENCE! I MEAN, ALL THINGS CONSIDERED, 4% OF THE VOTE IS PRETTY AMAZING!

YEAH, I MUST HAVE **SWEPT** MY IMMEDIATE CIRCLE OF FRIENDS!

HEY!— THAT'S AS VALID A POWER BASE AS THERE IS!

GBTrudeau

JEANIE, SOME-
THING'S BEEN
BOTHERING YOU
ALL DAY. I CAN
TELL. YOU'VE
GOT THAT...

HARRY, WE
CAN'T GO TO
THAT CLASS DIN-
NER TONIGHT.
RAY DELANEY
WILL BE THERE.

RAY DELANEY?! WELL,
OF **COURSE** HE'LL BE
THERE! HE WAS MY
ROOMMATE! AND I
THOUGHT YOU LIKED
HIM!

I DO, HARRY.
BUT MORE
THAN YOU
KNOW. LAST
YEAR WE HAD
AN AFFAIR.

JEANIE! YOU...YOU
REALLY HAD AN
AFFAIR?! THEN WE'VE
..WE'VE..FINALLY
ACHIEVED **PARITY!**

LOOKS
THAT WAY,
HARRY.

OH, THANK **GOD!** I
CAN'T **TELL** YOU HOW
THAT THING WITH
THE SITTER RIPPED
ME APART!

I KNOW,
HARRY. THAT
WAS ROUGH
ON YOU.